CLASSIC VARIATIONS

The Mysteries dramatises two of the greatest stories of Western European culture: the creation of the world and the life and death of Jesus Christ. Originally created by and for local communities during the fourteenth century, these cycles of dramatised stories offer an invaluable insight into the medieval world before Shakespeare.

This new version, drawing on texts from a wide variety of sources, retains the muscular and poetic language of the originals. It has been prepared by Edward Kemp working in close collaboration with the director of the Royal Shakespeare Company production, Katie Mitchell. The text is published in two volumes, *The Creation* and *The Passion*. Each volume carries an informed and informative introduction by Edward Kemp.

DRAMA CLASSICS   *titles in print*

Anon	*Everyman*
Aristophanes	*Lysistrata*
Büchner	*Woyzeck*
Chekhov	*Three Sisters*
Congreve	*The Way of the World*
Euripides	*Medea*
Farquhar	*The Beaux Stratagem*
Ibsen	*A Doll's House*
Ibsen	*Hedda Gabler*
Jonson	*The Alchemist*
Jonson	*The Devil is an Ass*
Jonson	*Volpone*
Labiche	*An Italian Straw Hat*
Marlowe	*Doctor Faustus*
Marlowe	*The Jew of Malta*
Molière	*The Hypochondriac*
Molière	*The Learned Ladies*
Sheridan	*The Rivals*
Strindberg	*Miss Julie*
Tourneur?	*The Revenger's Tragedy*
Webster	*The Duchess of Malfi*
Webster	*The White Devil*
Wilde	*The Importance of Being Earnest*

CLASSIC VARIATIONS

THE
MYSTERIES

Part One: The Creation

a new version by Edward Kemp
for the RSC production by Katie Mitchell

NICK HERN BOOKS
London

A Nick Hern Book

This version of *The Mysteries* (*Part I: The Creation*) first published
in Great Britain as a paperback original in 1997
by Nick Hern Books Limited, 14 Larden Road, London W3 7ST.

Typeset by Country Setting, Woodchurch, Kent TN26 3TB
Printed by Watkiss Studios Limited, Biggleswade SG18 9ST

A CIP catalogue record for this book is available from the British
Library

ISBN 1 85459 391 9

Introduction

The Mysteries began as a conversation between Katie Mitchell and myself in 1991. Katie through her experience of the Gardzienice theatre in Poland had begun to explore the relationship between theatre and folk culture, and from there she had developed an interest in pre-Reformation English culture. For my part, I was concerned with the notion of what it meant to be English at a time when other parts of the British Isles were asserting their identity (and non-Englishness) ever more dynamically; and as a theatre writer I was searching for a language that had the sheer rhythmic and poetic vigour of the Scots, Irish and North American writing that excited me. These two interests found a connection in the medieval English mystery cycles and we laid a plan to try to stage as fully and faithfully as possible one of these cycles in all the richness of its original language.

The plan, despite sporadic stirrings, remained unhatched until Adrian Noble invited Katie to become director of The Other Place in the winter of 1995/96. At this point we more or less picked up the idea as we had left it five years previously, though the venue was perhaps smaller and more conventionally theatrical than the one we had envisaged.

Of the twenty to thirty English mystery cycles for which records exist, only four have survived anything like intact. These are York, Chester, Towneley (almost certainly from Wakefield) and a manuscript known as 'N-Town' (previously called both the 'Ludus Coventriae' and the 'Lincoln cycle', but probably from Norfolk). Of these York is the most comprehensive and extensive in its telling of the standard mystery cycle of Creation to Passion to Doomsday. It is also linguistically very close to the Towneley cycle which features at least five plays by the so-called 'Wakefield Master', one of the great writers of pre-Reformation theatre. It is therefore quite possible to mix-and-match from York (which has some key passages missing) and Towneley to produce a thrilling over-view of much of the best of medieval English mystery play writing. This, *very* loosely, is what Tony Harrison did for the National Theatre in 1980s. At the beginning of 1996 our plans were not much different. I had seen Harrison's version in Bill Bryden's landmark production and I had got totally high on the language; this, a desire to present a coherent cycle, and my familial associations with York and Yorkshire, were enough to head us towards a York/Towneley confection.

I was to be employed, not as a writer or adapter but as dramaturg. I was to be the writers' representative (and there are a great many of them, all anonymous) in the rehearsal room, trying to get the plays on to the stage in as untampered a form as was commensurate with comprehensibility and changing theatrical times: our audience might be less than fluent with Middle English (although it is more comprehensible acted than read) and our small studio space might not be able to deliver all staging devices of a medieval pageant. To fulfil this role it became essential to try and get inside the heads of the people who made these plays: for me the problem reading the plays was not *what* was being said (an English degree had prepared me for the linguistic problems) but *why* it had been written.

There is a prevalent myth that the cycles, perhaps the begin-
nings of secular theatre in this country, were the creation of
the working classes. This is to look at the medieval period
through post-industrial spectacles. If one had to render the
situation in twentieth-century terms it might be as accurate
to describe the pageants as conceived and performed by the
intelligentsia and the middle classes, with skilled manual
workers employed to produce scenery and costumes; the
shop-floor maybe filled in the smaller roles and were the audience. But this is itself highly speculative. The more we have
worked on the project the clearer it has become to us that
what is really known about these plays consists of tiny fragments, from which each excavator has tried to reconstruct
some idea of the original, but in every case the resulting
image is composed of more reconstruction than fragments.

The one aspect that does seem fairly certain is that the
pageants were vast communal undertakings. Perhaps if one
could begin to understand the ties that bound a medieval
community together, that enabled, even encouraged a whole
city to come together annually in a religio-theatrical
adventure of considerable expense and effort, how the
attitude of a shipwright to his work was changed by playing
Noah, then maybe one could come to a wider understanding
of how communities can be built and labour valued in our
own age when patterns of both are changing radically. What
might a pre-industrial age teach us about living in a post-
industrial age?

So in the spring of 1996 we began a reading programme –
not only of the four cycles and fragments of cycles – but also
of a vast range of material, both medieval and contemporary,
that might guide us through the mind-set of the people who

made these plays and the culture in which they lived. By the autumn, when Katie, Vicki Mortimer and I became free of other commitments, I was able to spot a passing reference to St Augustine's interpretation of the Creation at twenty paces and Katie could enumerate all the Old Testament *figurae* fulfilled in the Crucifixion.

Our reading had shaken up the project in various ways. Contact with the other cycles had relieved us of a feeling of loyalty to any one cycle in particular. N-Town had become more and more attractive, initially for no better reason than that it has been so persistently overlooked or denigrated in academic literature. It had revealed itself to be highly suitable to our situation. The play seems to be made up of three separate elements: a two-part passion play, a play on the life of the Virgin Mary, and around them some bits and pieces assembled apparently to make the whole conform to a mystery cycle structure. Because much of it is written as coherent drama, as opposed to a series of discrete pageant scenes, it seemed much better suited to a static staging in a studio space. The language, though there are a great many passages of limpid poetry, lacks the wilder, alliterative invention of the northern cycles, and so is often more accessible to a modern ear. Also, through the Mary play and a greater space afforded to the female characters in the life of Jesus, there seemed for us an opportunity to balance the otherwise rather male-heavy narrative.

We had also learnt that N-Town is not alone in being a compilation rather than an integrated whole. Records suggest that mystery plays were being performed in Britain from the late fourteenth century until sometime in the mid-sixteenth century, yet in the case of York, N-Town and Towneley the manuscripts we have date from the latter part of the fifteenth century – that is, fifty to a hundred years before the plays ceased being performed. The York manuscript (which is possibly a prompt book or civic catalogue of the pageant) appears to record a number of changes being made to the plays; the Towneley script has several elements in common with York, as if they were in some way connected, perhaps drawing on the same lost original. So what has come down to us is less an authorised version, more a snapshot of the plays at one moment in their development, with little or no indication of their origins, or what form they took when they ceased performance. Armed with this knowledge we became fearless in borrowing from all the cycles in order to create our own compilation. It seemed no more than what the writers of the middle ages – eminently practical artisans – would have done. It also led to us exploring the mystery cycles of other countries. N-Town is decidedly more continental in feel than the Northern cycles, perhaps because it is more passion play than pageant cycle. The Cornish *Ordinalia* (and its late sixteenth-century re-working) has directly and indirectly influenced our script, especially in the story of Seth and the Oil of Mercy; there is also a certain minor influence from some of the mammoth French *mystères*.

Meanwhile, through the process of auditions and casting, it had become clear that to ask an actor to stand up and play 'I'm a medieval shipbuilder pretending to be Noah' was not a path we had any wish to pursue. Theatre rarely shows its snobbery more than when it presents 'non-actors' acting. To interpose a medieval personality between the actor's own and these astonishing mythic figures, seemed not only an unnecessary 'head-fuck' (Katie's term) but also in some way fraudulent: isn't the problem of 'I'm a man in the middle of the desert whom God has told to build a gigantic wooden box to save my family from flood' sufficient?

This was the point we had reached when Katie, Vicki and I set aside a weekend in Yorkshire to consider the project. We read a lot; we went into York and walked the route of the pageant (though significantly we spent more time in book-shops looking at Käthe Kollwitz monographs); we met with Peter Meredith of Leeds University, one of the most cogent of commentators on N-Town, who has been involved in several academic reconstructions of medieval plays, including the mystery cycles. Somewhere in the midst of all this, we also asked ourselves '*Why* are *we* doing this project *now?*' and found the answers we had been coasting on for five years no longer fitted the question. It seemed that we were in danger of building some quaint medieval time-capsule at the end of the millenium, inevitably compromised by lack of knowledge, indubitably coloured by twentieth-century prejudice. A piece of heritage theatre, perhaps entertaining in the shallowest sense, but devoid of any attempt fully to engage either with the material or with our audience: both abandoned behind an opaque barrier of medievalism.

So, two months before we began rehearsals, we started to reconstruct the project from the bottom up, determined that from now on we would work solely with the question *Why?* and trust that this, shaped by the already determined conditions of time and place, would lead us to *How?* We quite quickly arrived at a new shared starting point which in truth had never been far away: the teaching and life of Jesus. We were interested in certain aspects of his message, as we saw it, and drew up a list of oppositions – altruism vs selfishness, responsibility vs irresponsibility, community vs individualism, spiritual vs material, nature/harmony vs technology/dissonance. These seemed to us issues that Jesus – in the sometimes lucid, sometimes riddling way that his teaching has come down to us – was trying to address: trying to draw a society away from the latter towards the former in each case; issues that were current to him and still seem pretty current now. That a man needed to say these things, that a society felt it necessary to kill him for saying them, but other members of that society felt his message to be sufficiently important to continue to promote it, even at the cost of their own lives: this seemed like a story worth telling, independent of whether we could commit to particular beliefs about the man's divinity.

So that gave us enough to work on for Part Two of the two-part event we had promised to the RSC and its audience, but what about Part One? We decided that we needed to provide some kind of context for this man. A context in part local – the beliefs he (and through him, we) inherited – but also a broader one: how did humanity get into a situation where we seem persistently as a species to progress away from a life in balance with the rest of creation to a life based on reckless exploitation of it? Were the stories of the creation and evolution of society that have come down to us in the Bible at all useful for talking about these issues? Back on the shelf went St Augustine, Thomas Aquinas and Glynne Wickham, down came Liberation Theology, Stephen Hawking and Richard Dawkins.

It should be stressed at this point that what we are making is a piece of theatre, not a philosophical tract. The tools of theatre are very simple – an actor, an audience and a space

– just as an artist's tools might be described as *simply* paint, something to paint with and something to paint on, yet in each case a high degree of complexity can be achieved. The ideas behind a piece of theatre transferred into this medium of explanatory prose can seem excessively bald and simplistic, because that is as they should be. We have struggled over and over again in this project to simplify material to the point where it is actable. This is not because actors are in any way simplistic or even unintellectual people, but their work is not to explain complex ideas, but to realise complex situations. Anyone who has experience of fractals will know that the most apparently innocuous mathematical formulae can release patterns of mind-boggling complexity. In the best theatre something of the same effect can be achieved: the same actors in the same situation working with the same basic intentions can produce, night after night, a bewildering diversity of 'results'.

With the scientists we looked back to the beginning of creation. The inconceivable moment when out of nothing came something. One recent theory runs roughly: 'In the beginning there was nothing. Then there was a flaw in the nothing, a mistake in nothingness, and the mistake became so super-heated that it exploded, and caused the Big Bang.' By being put into words what is an elegant mathematical proposition swiftly becomes a surreal metaphor. Then how might we *stage* such an event? All we have is actors and a space and the audience's imagination. Might the right actor simply speaking the words of the Bible in the right setting bring us anywhere close? If we accept the Genesis accounts as a metaphor (which most people in our culture do) what does that acceptance of *this* metaphor, as opposed to any other Creation myth, tell us about the forces which shaped our culture? Liberation theology will tell us that it is vitally important to remember that God made creation and that it was *good*: isn't the essential goodness of creation, of nature, and for that matter of ourselves, something worth remembering? And physics will tell us that we and the universe are all made of the same stuff. We cannot conclusively claim the same maker, but we are all shaped from the same material as the stars.

We also at this time stumbled upon Jack Miles' remarkable book, *God − A biography*. By the apparently simple device of treating the Old Testament like a work of fiction in which God is the central character, Miles subtly reveals all the shifts and tensions that lie in the relationship between that character and his mirror image, humanity: his wilful but oh so adored offspring. This gave us the 'through line', the backbone of Part One that we had hitherto been missing.

It also sent us back to the Bible, and we became eager to try achieve in the script something of the stripped-back nature of the Bible stories themselves. In the mystery cycles it's often hard to move without banging one's head against a bulwark of Catholic propaganda, stubbing one's toe on some ill-informed piece of anti-Semitism. We became more and more rigorous about removing material that did not have biblical support, peeling off from the Old Testament our Christian interpretation of the stories: out went the Fall of Angels, out went Satan (who only makes two appearances in the Old Testament and neither of them in the Garden of Eden), out went any notion of hell. In tandem with this stripping-back to the source, we also examined the apocryphal stories which, though barred from the New Testament proper, had a major influence on medieval views of the birth and life of Christ. A meeting with an Islamic scholar directed our interest towards the Koran, where we were astonished (shamefully) at the closeness of some of the stories. The appearance of Adam, Noah and Abraham we might have expected, but to find Moses and Jesus held in such esteem, the latter even the product of a virgin birth, for this our culture had left us unprepared. From the start, we had been keen to avoid alienating non-Christian members of our audience: de-Christianising (or de-Judaising) the Old Testament might build one set of bridges; consideration of the Islamic versions of the same stories might provide another.

Having been passed through all these mills and meshes the material has, at the time of writing, also undergone the rigours of five weeks in the rehearsal room. It has shed a third of its length, but is, if anything, more radical in its manipulation of the story than the script which was first presented to the cast. Katie and I, having at the eleventh hour backed down from some of our more extreme positions, have been able to re-embrace them with the support of a remarkably courageous and generous company of actors.

The question could well be asked, in what sense does the place at which we have now arrived have any connection to the medieval mystery cycles which were our starting point? The majority of the text is still drawn from some medieval source or other. The choice to leave the language in a slightly simplified version of the original Middle English (with material from other sources being 'middle englished' to fit) is more than just a hang-over from our original starting point. I am still uncertain what kind of language one could use to tell these stories today. The King James Bible carries an immense cultural baggage of exactly the kind we found we needed to shed, and has the disadvantage of not being written for the theatre; also much of its most exquisite poetry turns out to be the result of slippery translation. In the twentieth century perhaps T.S. Eliot has made the most considered effort to find a language to write about spiritual issues, and it can hardly be coincidental that he leans towards exactly the kind of four-stress line that is the staple of the mystery cycle verse. Personally, I am still quite engaged by this strange hybrid in which our plays are now written, but I suspect the dialogue over the language will continue long through the run of the show.

The language issue aside, my hope (naive probably) is that the medieval writers and theologians who birthed these plays would at least understand the mind-set with which we have approached the project; that, having begun as their repre-sentative in the rehearsal room, they would not feel I have travestied their work wilfully. The problem is, simply, that the answers of faith to which they could appeal five hundred years ago are perhaps not ones we can use so readily now, or if they are, we have to approach them from a new direction. I do not think we have been patronising in our attitude to their work, we would never claim to understand more about the spiritual life of humanity than those great thinkers who devoted their lives to its contemplation. We do, however, as a society, know a good deal more about the material world, and that we cannot avoid: we cannot unthink what has been thought, or undiscover what has been discovered. Our quasi-anthropological investigation into medieval society, and what it might teach us about society now is not a project we have abandoned, but if we were to tackle it we would require material that gave us more ideological room for manoeuvre. By the by, it should be pointed out that the simplicity of our staging is probably not at all medieval. The taste of that time seems to have been very much for high tech spectacle – and if the historical records are anything to go by they were quite capable of achieving scenic effects which would turn Sir Cameron Macintosh green with envy (and appal any Health and Safety officer).

The relationship of a script to a stage production is complex, not least because theatre has never evolved an intricate method of record-keeping, unlike choreography or composition. I have not attempted here to describe what is happening on stage in the production. This is largely because at this point in rehearsals I simply do not know, and in any case the staging is likely to change in the long run of performances ahead, which will take it to four different theatres. Any precise documentation of the production as finished product will need to wait until it is finished (currently May 1998), and cannot be within the remit of this publication. The 'stage directions' are usually those which were originally presented to the company and are based largely on scriptural sources. They are often deliberately provocative, and should be considered to reflect the mood or ideas behind what is happening on stage rather than being a precise description of the action – the *why* rather than the *how*. Yet such is the transient nature of theatre work, that this script, only one small part of the overall undertaking, will, more than likely, outlast the production which gives it its relevance. I would like therefore to take the space here to pay credit to all those listed below whose work on the production has been at least as influential as my own, but whose efforts may not be immediately evident in the text that follows. Above all, I owe an enormous debt to Katie Mitchell. Her intelligence and imagination have shaped this script as much as anyone's; without her vision none of us would have gathered in the first place, and without her tireless questing we would have long ago foundered.

Edward Kemp
Stratford-upon-Avon, December 1996

Sources

It would be tedious to identify in detail the sources of all that follows. On occasion a quatrain may be made up of lines from all four cycles. Sections from the *Ordinalia* and Cornish *Creacion of the World* appear in my own free translations. My hand also lies behind a certain amount of material of biblical or apocryphal origin which the medieval writers had not provided us with, and in certain bridging sections. We have tried to invent nothing; that is, there is some kind of source for everything. This may seem like a meaningless restriction when so much of the process has been about manipulating and editing material to our ends, but because the field of inquiry is so vast we have had, at least in this initial stage, to impose some kind of boundary. The subject is so full of mystery and whim already, it seemed we should restrict our own in some way, however arbitrary. As David Ryall is fond of saying in rehearsals, 'There's too much mystery around today, what we need is *clarity*'.

The major sources are as follows:

Plays

The Chester Mystery Cycle, ed. R.M. Lumiansky and David Mills (Early English Text Society, 1986).

The Creacion of the World, ed. P. Neuss (New York and London, 1983).

The N-Town Play, ed. Stephen Spector (EETS, 1991).

Ordinalia: the Ancient Cornish Drama, ed. and trans. E. Norris (Oxford, 1859).

The Towneley Plays, ed. Martin Stevens and A.C. Cawley (EETS, 1994).

The York Plays, ed. Richard Beadle (Edward Arnold, 1982).

Scripture

The New Jerusalem Bible (Darton, Longman and Todd, 1985).

The Koran, trans. N.J. Dawood (Penguin, 1995).

The Apocryphal New Testament, ed. J.K. Elliott (Oxford, 1993).

THE MYSTERIES

Part One: The Creation

Acting Company

Josette Bushell-Mingo
Declan Conlon
Paul Hamilton
Paul Hilton
Kristin Hutchinson
Johnny Lodi
Richard Lynch
Myra McFadyen
Christopher Middleton
Ruth Mitchell
Joseph Mydell
Peter Needham
David Ryall
Tristan Sturrock
Edward Woodall

Directed by Katie Mitchell
Designed by Vicki Mortimer
Costumes co-designed by
   Johanna Coe

Lighting designed by
   Paule Constable
Music Ben Livingstone
Movement by Emma Rice
Fights by Nick Hall

Sound by Andrea J. Cox
Costume Supervisor
   Johanna Coe
Production Manager
   Mark Graham
Company voice work by
   Andrew Wade and
   Lyn Darnley

Stage Manager
   Michael Budmani
Deputy Stage Manager
   Lynda Snowden
Assistant Stage Manager
   Anna Hill

First performance of this production: The Other Place, Stratford-upon-Avon, 8 January 1997.

Creation

A formless void with darkness over the deep. A divine wind sweeps over the waters.

GOD. Let there be light.

There is light. GOD *sees that the light is good. He divides the light from darkness.*

GOD *(to the light).* Day.
                              (To the darkness.) Night.

Evening comes, morning comes: the first day.

Let there be a vault in the waters, even
In their midst, to divide them.

And so it is.

GOD *(to the vault).*   Heaven.

Evening comes, morning comes: the second day.

Let the waters under heaven here
Come together and let dry land appear.

And so it is.

The dryness 'earth' I call;
'Seas' the gathering of waters all.

GOD *sees that it is good.*

Let on earth plants spring,
Trees that flourish and fruit forth bring,

Each after their own kind.

And so it is. GOD *sees that it is good. Evening comes, morning comes: the third day.*

Let there be lights in heaven's height,
To divide the day from night;
So seasons, days and years be signed.
The greater light I call 'the sun'
And over day its rule shall run.
The lesser 'moon' and 'stars' I call,
And they the night well govern shall.

And so it is. GOD *sees that it is good. Evening comes, morning comes: the fourth day.*

Let the waters life forth bring:
Birds in the vault of heaven flying,
Great whales in the sea swimming.
Have these all My blessing.

And so it is. GOD *sees that it is good.*

Be fruitful all and multiply:
Fill now both the seas and sky.

Evening comes. Morning comes. The fifth day.

Let earth foster and forth bring
Every kind of living thing:
With beasts that move or creep on ground,
Now bid I that the earth abound.

And so it is. GOD *sees that it is good.*

Let Us make man in Our likeness,
To master this world both more and less.

GOD *shapes* ADAM *and* EVE *from the soil of the ground, in the image of Himself and blows the breath of life into their nostrils and they become living beings.*

Rise up, thou earth, rise up, rise,
And come with Me to paradise.

GOD *settles* ADAM *and* EVE *in the middle of the Garden of Eden where there are two trees: the Tree of Life and the Tree of the Knowledge of Good and Evil.*

Adam and Eve, this is the place
That I have made you by My grace;
In this Garden shall ye dwell.
Herbs, spice, fruit on tree,
Beasts, birds, all that ye see
Shall bow to you. Keep them well:
Your subjects shall they be.

Of all the trees in paradise,
May ye eat in your best wise.
But the Tree of Good and Ill,
What time you eat of this
Thou speeds thyself to spill,
And be brought out of bliss.
Adam and Eve, this tree alone
Within the Garden out-take I;
The fruit of it nigh it none,
For if ye do, then shall ye die.

At heaven and earth first I began
And six days wrought ere I would rest;
My work is ended now at man,
All likes Me well, but this is best.
The seventh day shall My resting be,

Thus will I cease, soothly to say,
My blessing with you always be;
Now to heaven I speed My way.

GOD *goes*.

Adam and Eve in Eden

ADAM. Eve, my fellow, how think thee this?

EVE. It is a place of joy and bliss
   That God has given to thee and me.

   The SNAKE *calls to them*.

SNAKE. Adam, Eve.

ADAM & EVE.   Who art thou?

SNAKE.   A friend.
   And for your good is the coming
   I hither sought.
   Of all the fruit that ye see hang
   In paradise, why eat ye nought?

ADAM. We may of them each one
   Take all that us good thought.

EVE. Save a tree out is ta'en,
   Would do harm to nigh it aught.

SNAKE. And why that tree, that would I wit,
   Anymore than all other by?

EVE. For our Lord God forbids us it,
   The fruit thereof, Adam nor I

To nigh it near.

ADAM. And if we did we both should die,
    He said and cease our solace here.

SNAKE. Yah, to me take tent;
    Take heed and thou shalt hear
    What the matter meant
    He moved in that manner.
    To eat thereof He you forfend
    I know it well, this was His skill:
    Because He would none other kenned
    These great virtues that long theretill.
    For will thou see,
    Who eats the fruit of good and ill
    Shall have knowing as well as He.

ADAM. Why, what kin thing art ye
    This tale to us doth tell?

SNAKE. A worm that wotteth well
    How ye may worshipped be.

EVE. What worship should we win thereby?
    To eat thereof us needeth it naught,
    We have lordship to make mastery
    Of all thing that here be wrought.

SNAKE. Do way!
    To greater state ye may be brought
    If ye will do as I shall say.

ADAM. To do is us full loath
    That should our God mispay.

SNAKE. Nay, certes, it is no wothe,
    Eat it safely ye may.

For peril right there none in lies,
But worship and great winning,
For right as God ye shall be wise
And peer to Him in all-kin thing.
Aye, gods shall ye be,
Of ill and good to have knowing,
For to be as wise as He.

ADAM & EVE. Is this sooth that thou says?

SNAKE. Yea, why trows thou not me?
I would by no-kins ways
Tell nought but truth to ye.

ADAM & EVE. Then will we to thy teaching take.

They eat the fruit. Their eyes are opened and they realise that they are naked.

EVE. Our fleshly eyes be all unlocked;
Naked now ourselves we see.

ADAM. That sorry fruit that we have sucked
To death has brought both thou and me.

EVE. Alas, that ever that speech was spoken
By wicked worm unto thee and me.
Our maker's bidding we have broken,
For we have touched His own dear tree.
Adam, lay this leaf on thy privity,
And with this leaf I shall hide me.

ADAM *and* EVE *hear the sound of* GOD *walking in the garden in the cool of the day.*

ADAM. I would full fain that hid were we,
From my Lord's sight – I wist not where.

They hide amongst the trees.

GOD. Adam, Eve. Where art thou there?

ADAM. Lord.

GOD.　　　　Why dost thou not come welcome Me?

ADAM. Because we are naked and all bare
We went to hide ourselves from Thee.

GOD. Who told thee that thou naked was,
O man that in Our image was made?
Lest thou has trespassed in this place,
And touched the tree that I forbade.

ADAM. The woman that was made by you,
She led me this deed to do.

EVE. Lord, when Thou wentest from this place,
A worm with a fair face
Said we should be full of grace,
The fruit if that we ate.

GOD. Thou wicked worm, woe worth thee ay,
For thou hast worked here such affray;
My curse on thee I set:
On thy gut shalt thou glide,
On earth shalt thou feed,
And enmity on every side,
Be between man and thy seed.
Man We made in Our likeness
As governor of great and less,
Since thou here this fruit hast ate,
A curse upon the earth I set,
Now shall ye ever swink and sweat,
And travail for your food;

Until the time thou turn once more
To the earth I took thee from before
For dust thou art, as well is seen,
And after this work, woe and pain,
To dust shalt thou return again,
And so shall all thy brood.
Travail shall they have from birth
And travail ever on the earth.
All they know shall be but dearth,
That once I gave such good.
For thou both hast done this deed,
Death hast thou brought to all thy seed.

ANGEL DEATH *appears.*

Justice, Mine angel bright,
To middle-earth go drive these two.

ANGEL JUSTICE *appears.*

ANGEL JUSTICE. All ready, Lord, as it is right,
Thy bidding bainly shall I do.
Ye wretches unkind and right unwise,
Out of this joy hie you in haste!
Your mirth is turned to careful sighs,
Your wealth with sin away is waste.

ANGEL JUSTICE *drives them from the Garden of Eden.*

GOD. Now man doth know as much as We,
To the Tree of Life I bar the way;
Lest they should once come nigh that tree,
Eat its fruit and live for ay.

Outside the Gates of Eden

EVE. The gates be shut with God's key.
   Put in paradise at prime of day,
   By eventide all lost have we;
   We wend as wretch in woesome way;
   In black bushes our bower shall be.
   Now stumble we on stalk and stone.
   My wit away is from me gone!
   Writhe onto my neckbone
   With hardness of thy hand.

ADAM. Lief woman, turn thy thought.
   I will not slay thee, we are one flesh,
   For of one clod our flesh was wrought.
   My weeping shall be long fresh,
   Short liking shall be long bought.
   Let us walk forth into the land,
   With right great labour our food to find,
   With delving and digging with mine hand,
   Our bliss to bale and care declined,
   Now come, go we hence.

As they walk the ground withers under their feet.

Death

ANGEL DEATH. I am sent from God; Death is my name.
   Both man, and beast, and birds wild and tame,
   Herb, grass, and trees strong, I take them all in-same.
   Though I be naked and poor of array
   And worms have gnawed me all about,

Yet look ye dread me night and day;
For when Death cometh ye stand in doubt.
Naked then shall ye be;
Amongst worms, as I you tell,
And they shall eat flesh and fell,
As they have done me.

The Earth

ADAM *digs and the earth cries; again he digs and again the earth cries.*

ADAM. Father of all, hear our cry:
　　Let the earth here open be,
　　That Eve and I before we die,
　　Some sustenance find might we

GOD. Open, earth, at My command,
　　By one full length of Adam's hand.

ADAM. Gracious Lord, this is too small:
　　All that comes from this we shall
　　Eat within one day.

GOD. Two hands lengths then here I give
　　To thou and Eve by which to live.

ADAM. Yet, Lord, I pray:
　　If offspring should from us proceed,
　　Such offspring might we never feed.

GOD. Take what thou will,

And ye may feed on all ye find.
The earth so grant I to thy kind,
The land to tend and till.

Cain and Abel

ABEL. Brother Cain, to God our friend
    Methinks we now our thanks should tend;
    To give Him part of our fee,
    Corn or sheep whether it be.

CAIN. Should I leave my field and all thing
    And now with thee make offering?
    What gives God thee to praise him so?
    He gives me naught but sorrow and woe.

ABEL. Cain, leave this vain carping,
    For God gives thee all thy living.

CAIN. Abel, God gives me scarce a thing!
    My winnings are but mean –
    No wonder if that I be lean –
    And I am each year worse than other;
    Here by my troth it is none other.
    When I should sow and wanted seed,
    And of corn had full great need,
    Then gave He me none of His;
    So will I give Him none of this.

ABEL. Our father Adam has us kenned
    How to God we should make tend.

CAIN. Yea, yea, thou jangles waste;
  Ill may me speed if I have haste
  To deal my good, or give
  Either to God or yet to man
  Of any good that ever I won.
  As long as I may live.

ABEL. Dear brother, it were great wonder
  That thou and I should go asunder,
  Then would our father have great woe.
  Are we not brothers, I and thou?

CAIN. Cry on, cry on, whiles thee think good!
  Here my troth, I hold thee wood.
  Whether God be blithe or wrath
  To share my wealth is me full loath.
  But well I see tend must I need.
  So tend thou first – ill might thou speed.

  ABEL *offers the first-born of his flock and some of their fat as well.*

ABEL. God that shaped both earth and heaven,
  I pray to Thee Thou hear my steven,
  And take in thank, if Thy will be,
  The tend I offer here to Thee;
  For I give it in good intent
  To Thee, my Lord, that all has sent.
  I offer it now, with steadfast thought,
  In worship of Thee that all has wrought.

CAIN. Rise, let me now, since thou has done.

  CAIN *offers some of the produce of the soil.*

  Lord of heaven, hear Thou my boon –
  Here before Thee mayst Thou see

Such corn as did grow to me.
Part of it I bring to Thee,
Anon without a let.
I hope Thou wilt requite me this
And send me more of worldly bliss;
Else forsooth Thou dost amiss
And Thou beest in my debt.

GOD *favours* ABEL's *sacrifice.*

ABEL. Ah, lief God and Lord of bliss,
　　Now soothly know I well by this
　　My sacrifice accepted is
　　Before Thy face today.

CAIN. His sacrifice I see God takes,
　　And mine refuses and forsakes.

GOD. Cain, why art thou so wrath? Why?
　　Thy semblance changes wondrously.
　　Wotst thou not well that for thy deed
　　If thou do well thou may have meed;
　　If thou do foul, then foul will speed
　　And surely ever after be.
　　But, Cain, thou shalt have all thy will,
　　Thy talent if thou wilt fulfill.

CAIN. Ah, well, well, is it so?
　　Come forth with me. Thou must go
　　Into the field a little fro;
　　I have an errand to pay.

ABEL. Dear brother, I would do thy will,
　　But I must fare the fields until,
　　Where our flocks do feed their fill –

CAIN. I say thee nay.
  God hath challenged me now here
  For thee, and thou shalt pay full dear;
  And die thou shalt this night.
  Though God Himself stood in this place
  For to help thee in this case,
  Thou should die before His face.
  Have this, and get thee right.

  CAIN *strikes* ABEL *and kills him.* DEATH *appears.*

GOD. Cain, where is thy brother Abel?

CAIN. I know not. I cannot tell.
  Of my brother, Thou wotst well,
  I never had the keeping.

  ABEL*'s blood cries for vengeance.*

GOD. What hast thou done, thou wicked man?
  Thy brother's blood calls thee upon
  Vengeance as fast as it can,
  From earth to Me crying.
  Cain, cursed on earth thou shalt be ay,
  For the deed that thou hast done today
  And wickedly hast wrought.
  To all men thou shalt be unlief,
  Idle and wand'ring as an thief
  And overall set at naught.

CAIN. Out, alas! Where may I go?
  Whoso I meet will have me slain,
  Each man on earth will be my foe.
  No grace to me may gain.

GOD. Nay, Cain, thou shalt not die soon,

That is not thy brother's boon,
Thy blood for to be shed.
Yea, indeed, who slayeth thee
Sevenfold punished shall he be;
I set My mark upon thy head,
That all men may thee know.

GOD *marks* CAIN *with* ABEL's *blood*.

And for that thou hast done this deed,
As thee shall suffer all thy seed,
Whilst they on earth may go.

CAIN. I am wholly without grace.
So will I go from place to place
And look where is the best.
Well I know what place come I
Each man will loathe my company;
So shall I never have rest.
But yet will I, ere I go,
Speak with my dam and sire also.
Curse me though they must.

CAIN *goes*.

Burial

GOD (*to* DEATH). Abel's blood doth sore offend Mine eye.
Go, thou, and scratch the earth around,
So man from thee might learn thereby.
To grave his body in the ground.

ABEL *is buried*.

CAIN *comes to* ADAM *and* EVE.

CAIN. Dam and sire, rest you well,
 For one foul tale I can you tell.
 I have slain my brother Abel
 As we fell in a strife.

ADAM. Alas, alas, is Abel dead?
 Alas, cruel Cain what hast thou said?
 My curse be ever on thy head.
 No joy is left in life.

EVE. Alas, is my son slain?
 Marred then is all my main,
 And I must never more be fain
 But in woe and mourning.
 Well I wot and know iwis
 That very vengeance this is,
 For we to God so did amiss,
 May we never more have liking.

CAIN. Yea, dam and sire, farewell ye;
 For out of land I will flee.
 I dare not here abide.
 Now will I wend my way
 To look where that I best may
 From man's sight me hide.

Seth

ADAM. Come hither, Seth, my son so fair,
 And hearken what I say to thee:
 In world have I lived nine hundred year,

But many more shall I not see.
Yet ere death comes to make my end,
Some grace of God I long to know:
For though we did Him sore offend,
Yet might He still some mercy show.
Go thou then to that good Garden:
Where an angel guards the gates full fast;
Ask her, as she is a wise warden,
If Oil of Mercy shall come at the last.

SETH. Father, I know not the way.

ADAM. Walk to the east, as well thou may.
   I trust that thou wilt know the trace:
   Where we did tread only ash is found;
   For as went we woeful from that place
   Our footsteps they did burn the ground.

SETH. Freely, father, for thy sake,
   This travel will I take.
   But first thy blessing would I crave.

ADAM. My blessing be ever thee upon;
   Go swiftly now, Seth my son,
   The good God may thee save.

   SETH *goes.*

At the gates of Eden. SETH *approaches.*

ANGEL JUSTICE. Seth, come near.
   Say what errand thou dost here,
   Thus far to fare.

SETH. My father, fair angel, grows faint and old:
   He would no longer wend on wold
   With mickel care.

To this stead he hath me sent,
To seek, ere his life be spent,
Some of the Oil of Mercy.

JUSTICE. Within the gate put thou thy head;
Behold all well, and without dread
Say what thou dost see.

SETH *looks through the gates.*

SETH. What I have seen no tongue may tell.
A garden green of such sweet smell,
Of sights so sheen and fair amell;
The like I never saw.
Four rivers flow, broad and bright,
From a fountain full of waters white;
Of silver song and seemly sight
There is a store.

JUSTICE. Say what further thou didst see.

SETH. In midst of garden I saw a tree,
Standing there,
Whose roots were deep in ground.
About the trunk a worm was wound;
The boughs were bare.
Another tree there stood nearby,
Its branches growing up on high:
All green and fair;
And in its height a maid I saw,
And in her arms a babe she bore,
All wrapped about.

JUSTICE. Well hast thou looked, O Adam's son.
That tree all bare it is the one,
Without a doubt,

That brought thy parents into woe;
The worm the same that taught them so,
To be cast out.
The Tree of Life thereby doth stand –
Which way I ward at God's command –
And thereon grow
The fruit from which shall mercy spring,
When gracious God who made all thing
His grace would show.

SETH. And shall that grace my father have
Ere he is dead and closed in grave?

JUSTICE. I tell thee no.
By time that thou hast homeward sped,
Thy father, Seth, he will be dead.
Yet hear my speech.
These seeds I give to thee,
From Tree of Life the fruit so free,
Do as I teach:
When Adam is laid in earth beneath,
Set thou between his tongue and teeth
These seeds each.
By this may mercy come to men,
If mercy they should ever ken.
And now be gone.

SETH. I thank thee, angel. I shall obey
And work all this as thou dost say,
Till it be done.

SETH *goes.* DEATH *comes to* ADAM.

ADAM. Ah, Death, dry is thy drift.
Dead is my destiny.

My head is cloven in a cleft;
For clap of care I cry;
Mine eyelids may I not lift;
My brain waxen empty.
I may not once my head up shift.

DEATH. Thou sees Death, Adam, to thee draw,
As Eve and Abel did before.
On earth thou set me by thy deed,
And now to earth thou shalt thee speed.

ADAM *dies.*

SETH *finds* ADAM*'s body.*

SETH. Dear father, thou lies here dead,
And I have lost a trusty friend,
The first of all our kindred.
Who shall my care now mend?
But I shall do as the angel taught,
And lay thee, father, in the ground.
For from the earth ye once were wrought,
So shall ye now in earth be bound.
I lay these seeds beneath thy tongue,
From which may spring a joyful tree;
Let many sorrowful songs be sung,
And pray that mercy we shall see.

Lamech

JABAL. Fair morning is it, father.

LAMECH.   Silence, thou knave.

Wanting of eyesight in pain doth me bind.

JABAL. Blindness doth make thy wit for to rave.

LAMECH. Great mourning I make, and great cause I have,
    For now I see not; for age am I blind.
    While I had sight there might never man find
    My peer of shooting in all this world about.
    For yet shot I never at hart, hare nor hind
    But that he died, of this have no doubt.
    Lamech, son of Cain, my name was overall,
    And by this sling was my fame ever spread.
    Record, my boy – or witness this ye shall –
    What mark that were set me, soon it were dead.

JABAL. It is true, father, what you say, betide;
    For in that time were thy sling in thy hand,
    And were your mark but half a mile wide,
    That mark would you hit – if nigh ye did stand.

LAMECH. I never failed what mark were me set
    While I might look and had my clear sight.
    And still methinketh, no man should shoot bett
    Than I should do now, if mine hand were set right.
    Aspy some mark, boy, my sling I pull tight,
    And set mine hand to shoot some beast.
    And I dare lay a wager his death for to dight.
    The mark shall I hit, my life do I hest.

JABAL. Under yon great bush, father, a beast do I see.
    Give me thine hand here and hold it full still.
    Now is thine hand even as ever it may be.
    Draw up thine tackle yon beast for to kill.

LAMECH. My sling shall I draw right with hearty will;
    This sharp stone I shoot, that beast to assail.

Now have at that bush yon beast for to spill.
Smartly I swap and I shall not fail.

CAIN *cries out as he dies.*

DEATH *appears.*

LAMECH. Hark, boy, come tell me the truth in certain,
What man is he that this cry doth thus make?

JABAL. Cain hast thou killed, I tell thee plain;
With thy sharp shooting his death doth he take.

LAMECH. Have I slain my father? Wretch wicked on wold,
God will be venged full sadly on me:
For death of Cain I shall have sevenfold
More pain than he had that Abel did slay.
Have I slain my father? Alas what have I done?
Thou stinking lurdeyn, thou hast this wrought.
Thou art the why I slew him so soon;
Therefore shall I kill thee here – thou scapest not.

He beats his son JABAL *to death.*

LAMECH. These two deaths full sore bought shall be:
Upon all my blood God will venge this deed.
Wherefore, sore weeping, hence will I flee,
And look where I may best my head soon hide.

Noah

NOAH *digging.*

NOAH. Why is the world beloved, that false is and vain,
Since that its wealths be uncertain?

As soon slideth his power away
As doth a brittle pot that fresh is and gay.
Trust ye rather to letters written in th'ice
Than to this wretched world, that full of sin is.
It is false in its behest and right deceiveable;
It hath beguiled many men, it is so unstable.
It is rather to believe the wavering wind
Than the changeable world, that maketh men blind.
I have six hundred years and odd,
Lived on earth, as any sod,
In grievance alway.
And now I wax old,
Sick, sorry and cold;
As muck upon mold
I wither away.

GOD. Noah, My friend, come walk with Me;
For I would speak with thee privily.
Methought I showed man love when I made him to be
All angels above, in the likeness of Me;
And now in great reproof full low lies he,
In earth himself to stuff with sin
It harms Me so hurtfully
That murder doth now multiply,
That each man works so wickedly
And kills his kin.
That ever I made man regret I full sore,
For by My love he sets no store,
So all shall perish, less and more.
I shall fordo all this middle-earth
With floods that shall flow with hideous wrath;
I have good cause thereto, for of Me no man is feared.
As I say shall I do; of vengeance draw My sword

And make end
Of all that bears life,
Save thou and thy wife,
For ye would never strive
With Me, nor Me offend.
So, Noah My friend, from cares thee to keel
An ark thou shape of boards full well.
Thou hast been to Me as true as steel,
And thus My friendship shall thou feel.

NOAH. Ah, Lord, Thy will shall ever be wrought,
But first, of carpentry can I nought,
Of this making have I no mark.

GOD. Noah, I bid thee heartly, have no thought,
I shall thee wis in all thy work,
And even till it to end be wrought;
Therefore to Me take heed and hark.
Three hundred cubits it shall be long
And fifty broad, all for thy bliss;
The height of thirty cubits strong,
Look leally that thou think on this.
Anoint the ark with pitch and tar,
This the water out to spar;
A door high on the side thou fit,
That water may not come nigh it.

NOAH. Lord, all shall be done as Thou would will;
But what worth should we work theretill?
If all this earth Thou would fordo,
Save me and mine − let us perish too.

GOD. Noah, My servant sad and clean,
My favour shall ever on thee fall;

Work My will and without ween
This work shall save thy kin withal.
When the ark is ordered so,
With diverse stalls and stages there,
Of every beast thou shall take two,
Male and female in a pair.
Thy wife and sons in with thee go
And their three wives, all without fear.
These eight bodies and no mo
Shall thus be saved in this manner.
Take with thee gear such as may gain
To man and beast, their lives to last.
Now to My bidding be thou bain,
Till all be harboured haste thee fast;
After the seventh day it shall rain
Till forty days be fully past.
On earth there shall be such a flood,
That every thing that hath life form,
Beast and body with bone and blood,
Shall all be stroyed through stress of storm,
Of all man's works I will take wrake;
They shall be sunken for their sin,
But thou shalt be saved for thy sake.
Therefore go boldly and begin.

NOAH. Ah, blissful Lord, that all may bield,
I thank Thee heartily both ever and ay;
Six hundred winters am I of eld –
Me think these years as yesterday.
Full weak I was and all unwield,
My weariness is went away,
To work this work here in this field
With all my fry I shall assay.

NOAH *and his family build the ark.*

NOAH. Go call your mother, and come near,
  And speed us fast that we not spill.

SHEM. Father, I am all ready here,
  Your bidding bainly to fulfill.

  SHEM *goes to get his mother.* TUBALCAIN *and* JUBAL
  arrive.

TUBALCAIN. Noah, hast thou thy five wits lost?
  What is this deed that here thou dost,
  To make this work of such great cost?
  What wouldst thou win?

NOAH. Friend Tubalcain, though now you smile,
  Ye shall weep within awhile,
  And many other men of guile,
  That are so sunk in sin.
  God that made both day and night,
  Who will wreak a reckoning right,
  To shape this ark He did me dight
  To save me and my kin.

JUBAL. Save thee? I am astound.

NOAH. All that go upon this ground,
  In fearsome floods shall soon be drowned,
  I tell thee this in truth.
  Although ye now may dance and drink,
  And little of God's love ye think,
  Soon I say ye all shall sink,
  For God will take no ruth.

TUBALCAIN. Noah, we are in midst of land,
  No water hereabouts doth stand,

    I swear to thee, by this hand,
    Thine ark will never float.

NOAH. For this world to amend,
    Such a flood God will send,
    Rain forty days without end,
    Until sin be smote.

JUBAL. Methinks thou waxest wood.
    On earth shall flow a fearsome flood?
    And thou alone and all thy brood
    Saved shall be?
    All waters which be in wide world's space,
    Be they gathered together in one place
    Would not bring such a bale to pass,
    I warrant thee.

TUBALCAIN. Ya, why should God that this world wrought
    Bring His building now to nought?
    How came this thinking in thy thought?
    Tell me – I pray you.

NOAH. By God's own word I understand:
    Since sin is so outspread in land,
    And no man here keeps His command,
    He will this world fordo.
    But if ye would atonement make,
    Your sinful ways full soon forsake,
    Such shriving may His sharpness slake,
    And so He might ye spare.

JUBAL. Thou ram's tout, who did thee teach,
    So prettily, bald pate, us to preach?
    When thou didst with great God have speech
    Was aught other there?

TUBALCAIN. A cat's fart care we for thy clatter.
    What canst thou, man, of any matter,
    That builds an ark to float on water?
    Such folly ne'er was seen.

NOAH. He that hath this whole world wrought,
    Both earth and heaven and all from nought,
    His power is mighty beyond thought,
    And His wrath is keen.

TUBALCAIN *and* JUBAL *go.*

SHEM *returns.*

SHEM. Father, I have done now as ye command,
    My mother comes to you this day.

NOAH. She is welcome, I well warrand;
    This world shall soon be wasted away.

NOAH's WIFE *comes into the ark.*

WIFE. Where art thou, Noah?

NOAH.   Lo, here at hand.
    Come hither fast, dame, I thee pray.

WIFE. Trows thou that we should leave the town
    And flit over these fells?

NOAH. Yea, certes, or we shall drown.

WIFE. I tell thee, Noah, set this down
    And come do somewhat else.

NOAH. Dame, seven days are duly past,
    And now it doth begin to rain.
    Alive shall no man longer last,
    But we alone. This is plain.

WIFE. Faith, Noah, thou grows fond full fast.
    I shall not fret on this refrain;
    Thou art near wood, I am aghast,
    Farewell, I will go home again.

NOAH. Oh, woman, art thou not wood?
    Of my works thou nought wit;
    All that has bone and blood
    Shall be overflowed with the flood.

WIFE. In faith, thou were as good
    To let me go my gate.

The WIFE *makes to go.*

NOAH. Help, my sons, to hold her here,
    For to her harms she takes no heed.

HAM. Come, mother, mend your cheer.
    All is sooth our father said:
    This world be drowned, without dread.

WIFE. Alas, that I this lore should hear.

NOAH. Thou spills us all if thou not speed.

JAPHETH. Dear mother, stay with us,
    Here nothing shall you grieve.

WIFE. Nay, nay, home I must,
    For I have tools to truss.

NOAH. Woman, why does thou thus?
    To make us more mischief?

WIFE. Noah, thou might have let me wit.
    Early and late thou went thereout,
    And ay at home thou let me sit

To look that nowhere were well about.

NOAH. Dame, thou hold me excused of it,
  It was God's will without doubt.

WIFE. And would thou wit my will?

NOAH. I pray thee, dame, be still.

HAM'S WIFE. Ah why fare ye thus,
  Father and mother both?

SHEM'S WIFE. Ye should not be so spitous,
  We stand in such wothe.

WIFE. Bairns, we will do as ye bid us,
  We will be no more wrath.

  They start to get into the ark.

NOAH. Great God, that all may spare or spill,
  We yield us now unto thy will.

  The door is closed.

  *The windows of heaven open. The waters rise until all the highest
  mountains under heaven are covered. Every living thing upon the face
  of the earth is destroyed. Inside the ark the family sings.*

  At length, silence. The waters subside. NOAH *opens the door of
  the ark, and the family come out.*

NOAH. Behold this plain,
  Neither cart nor plough
  Doth here remain:
  Neither tree nor bough,
  Nor other thing.
  But all is away.
  Many dwelling, I say,

And much great array
Flit has this flowing.
Lord God such grace has granted we
Where all was lost, safe to be!
Therefore are we bound –
Wife, sons and your three wives –
To honour Him who spared our lives,
Here upon this mound.

The family build an altar where a small shoot is sprouting out of
ADAM's skull, and present burnt offerings. GOD smells the
pleasing smell.

GOD. Noah, to Me thou art full able
And thy offering acceptable
For I have found thee true and stable;
With thee man begins anew.
Ye shall now grow and multiply,
The earth again to edify.
Each beast and fish and fowl that fly
Shall be afeared of you.
Whereas ye did eat before
Trees and roots since ye were bore,
Of clean beasts now, less and more,
I give thee leave to eat.
But flesh that has yet blood within
I bar to thee and all thy skin;
So shall ye leave such meat.
Manslaughter must ye also flee:
They that shed blood, he or she,
That blood foul shed shall be
And vengeance have, men shall see.
Go forth now, the earth to fill.

NOAH. What worth is it to work and till,
    If Thou may ever at Thy will
    Such vengeance as this take?

GOD. Noah, I promise Thee before,
    Such vengeance shall I seek no more.

NOAH. To the mighty promises are no law,
    In wrath they may them break.

GOD. Noah, this covenant shall not be broken.
    Lo, here I send to thee a token,
    That it shall be as I have spoken:
    My bow between you and Me
    In the heavens here shall be
    By this sign you may see
    Such vengeance here doth cease,
    And man and God shall be at peace.

    ANGEL PEACE *appears.* GOD *sets his bow in the clouds.*

Abraham

GOD. Abraham, Abraham.

ABRAHAM. Who art thou?

GOD.   It is I, take tent to Me,
    That formed thy father Adam
    And everything in its degree.

ABRAHAM. To hear Thy will, ready I am;
    Whate'er it be it shall be done.

GOD. If thou Me love, then take thy son

Him thou holdest most of price,
And slay him as a sacrifice.

ABRAHAM. I had rather, if Thou it pleased,
 That Ye should waste all good I have,
 Or that myself should be deceased,
 So Thou, God, my son might save.
 I love my child as my life;
 Yet I love my God much more,
 And though my heart does make much strife,
 I must do after Thy lore.

 GOD *goes*.

My sweet son, come to me now.

Abraham's only SON *comes to him.*

SON. All ready, father. What willst thou?

ABRAHAM. Loves thou me, son, as thou hast said?

SON. Yea, father, with all mine heart,
 More than all that ever was made.

ABRAHAM. So I love thee, for my part.
 Come kiss me here, for true love's sake.

SON. At your bidding your mouth I kiss.

 The SON *kisses his* FATHER.

ABRAHAM. Now, son, we must an offering make,
 God himself has bad us this.
 Go, my child, set here at hand
 My knife and all that needs theretill.

SON. To work our dear Lord's own command,
 I am ever, father, at thy will.

ABRAHAM. Look thou miss nought that we should need.

SON. I am full ready to do this deed.

> SON *goes to get the knife.*

ABRAHAM. Alone, right here upon this hill,
Might I weep till my heart bust.
I would all were well with my full will,
But it must needs be done at last.

> SON *brings the knife to* ABRAHAM, *who starts to sharpen it.*

SON. Father, what will ye sacrifice?
To know your tend I am full fain,
That it be done in the best wise.

ABRAHAM. God above shall it ordain.

SON. A live beast, wot I, must be dead,
A righteous sacrifice to make.

ABRAHAM. Fear not, our Lord, as I have said
Will send some beast for us to take.

SON. Why thine knife dost thou sharpen so?

> ABRAHAM *weeps.*

SON. Let be, good father, cease your woe;
Or tell me what doth grieve thee sore,
That I might seek some help therefore.
Dear father, I pray you, hide not from me,
But some of your thought tell your son.

ABRAHAM. Ah, son, son, I must kill thee.

SON. Kill me, father? What have I done?

ABRAHAM. I tell thee, truly none ill.

SON. And shall be slain?

ABRAHAM.   So have I het.

SON. What may help?

ABRAHAM.   Certes, no skill.

SON. I ask mercy.

ABRAHAM.   That may not let.

SON. What have I done, father, what have I said?

ABRAHAM. Truly no-kins ill to me.

SON. And thus guiltless shall be arrayed.

ABRAHAM. Or much displeased our Lord will be.
　　It is His commandment and His will
　　That I my only son should kill.

SON. God's will? Nay, then, father, let it not be
　　That ye should grieve Him e'er for me.
　　God's own word we may not scorn,
　　So am I ready to be slain.
　　I pray thee, father, do not mourn,
　　But to His bidding be thou bain.

ABRAHAM. My son, my son, my blessing on thee.

　　ABRAHAM *binds his* SON.

SON. The shining of your bright blade
　　It makes me quake with fear to die.

ABRAHAM. Therefore downwards thou shalt be laid,
　　And when I strike thou shalt not see.
　　Farewell, my son, I shall thee yield
　　To Him that all this world might shield.

SON. When I am dead and closed in clay
    Who shall then your son be?

ABRAHAM. Speak no such words, I thee pray.

SON. I love thee ay.

ABRAHAM.   So do I thee.

*ABRAHAM stretches out his hand and takes the knife to kill his
SON.*

The ANGEL MERCY/GABRIEL *appears.*

MERCY. Abraham! Abraham!

ABRAHAM.   Who is there now?

MERCY. Against the boy raise not thy hand.

ABRAHAM. Say, who bad so? Any but thou?

MERCY. Yea, it is God's own command.
    He has perceived thy love in this
    And obedience to his law, iwis:
    He will thou do thy son no distress.
    For He has grant to thee His bliss.

ABRAHAM. But wot thou well that it is
    As thou has said?

MERCY.   I say thee yes.

ABRAHAM. To speak with thee I have no space,
    With my dear son till I have spoken.
    My good son, thou shalt have grace.
    Rise up.

SON. Shall I live?

ABRAHAM.   Yea, this is token.

ABRAHAM *kisses his* SON.

SON. Will God not send us mickel strife?

ABRAHAM. Nay, He Himself has grant thy life.

MERCY. Hark, Abraham, and take good heed.
For by Himself God has this sworn:
Because thou wouldst have done this deed,
All shall be saved that were forlorn;
For to His word thou didst obey,
All men on earth, as I thee say,
Shall be saved through thy seed.

ABRAHAM. Gramercy, Lord and king of grace,
That shows Thy mercy in this place.

Moses

MOSES *in the wilderness. He has a speech impediment.*

MOSES. Lord, oft our fathers have us told
How Seth did make a journey bold
To where the gates of Eden stand.
How he did see that peerless place,
That fair garden of Thy grace,
Whence we be barred with many band.
How it were promised to him then
That mercy should be shown to men.
Yet many thousand year be gone:
Noah, Abraham and all their fry
Who hoped Thy mercy would them buy,
Are dead, their deeds are done;

And still we dwell upon the earth
With mickel care and doleful dearth,
And sin spreads far and free.
If Ye would but Thy mercy show,
That man might thus Thy glory know,
So should they turn again to Thee.
Let us the Oil of Mercy see.

GOD *appears.*

GOD. Moses! Moses!

MOSES.   I am here.

MOSES *approaches.*

GOD. Come not too near,
But hearken unto Me a space.
Do off thy shoes as thou stands there,
For full holy is this place.

MOSES. Now my shoes are from my feet;
Barefoot before Thee do I stand.

GOD. Approach then, Moses, with Me to meet,
These tablets I give thee in thine hand.
With My finger on them is writ
All My laws, thou understand.
Look that ye hold them nought
For trifles nor for fables;
For ye do well to understand,
That I wrote them with My own hand
In these same tables.
The first commandment to you I say:
Make no god of stick or stone
And trow in no god but one,

Who made both night and day.
Understand well what meaneth this,
Every man in his degree,
And never set your heart amiss
Upon worldly vanity.
For if thou set thy love so sore
Upon riches and worldly good,
Thy worldly riches takest thou ever more
Even for thy god, as no man should.
The second bids thou shalt not swear,
For no meed nor for no dare,
Falsely by My name.
If thou swear wrongfully,
Wit thou well and witterly,
Thou art worthy great blame.
The third commandment, as I say,
Bids thee hallow the seventh day.
For in six days this world I made.
And care not much for rich array,
For right poor man in ragged weed,
Better than rich in garments gay
May oft this commandment heed.
The fourth command says to thee all:
Father and mother worship thou shall.
Though that your parents may be poor,
And thou a store of gold and good,
Yet look ye worship them the more,
From whom thou hast both flesh and blood.
The fifth commands thou shalt not slay
Any man, for gold nor pay.
Not for love, nor for hate.
The sixth: fornication thou shalt forsake,

And rather a spouse to thee shall take
And always live in righteous state.
The seventh commands thou shalt leave,
And neither go to steal nor thieve,
Not for more or less.
The eighth bids both the old and young
That be true of their tongue
And bear no false witness.
The ninth command to dam and sire,
Thy neighbour's spouse shalt thou not desire;
But keep to thine own choice.
The tenth command, and last, is this:
Desire thee not thy neighbour's house,
Nor anything that is his.
These be the laws that ye must keep.
Therefore every one set well in mind,
Whether ye do wake or sleep,
These laws to learn be not behind.
All about look that thou preach;
Whoso to God a friend would be,
To these laws now bend they each,
That they be kept in all degree.

MOSES. Me? Lord, no man my words will hear,
For all the oaths that I may swear.
To name such note of new
As this Thy commandment,
Some other best were to do,
To me no man will take intent.

GOD. Moses, be not abashed
My bidding boldly to bear.
In thee I put My trust

And shall keep thee from all care.
Go forth and preach anon, and see
That thou not cease nor night nor day.

MOSES. By Your law shall all judged be;
Your will to work I walk my way.

MOSES *goes.*

The Parliament of Heaven

The four ANGELS *come to* GOD. DEATH *holds pieces of the broken tablets.*

DEATH. Lord, Death comes here to speak for truth.
See, how man doth keep Thy Law.
These unkind creatures show no ruth,
But they will ever grieve Thee sore.

JUSTICE. The first of man that ever Thou made,
Turned full fast from Thee towards ill;
But one tree Thou them forbade,
Yet they scorned Thy love and broke Thy will.

DEATH. Cain thou loved, yet he slew his brother;
And many that same path have trod.
Sin and slaughter above all other
Have they taken for their God.

MERCY. Remember the promise made to Seth,
That Oil of Mercy man should know;
Shall man, Thy love, live in the shadow of death,
And never Thy loving mercy know?

JUSTICE. To see such mercy be they fit?
    When Thou did send a fearsome flood,
    That all with life away were flit,
    Did man thereafter turn to good?
    Learned they aught of Thy great main?
    Nay, they turned again to ill.
    Let them ever dwell in woe and pain
    For they will never keep Thy will.

PEACE. But to Noah Thou hast promised peace,
    Twixt Thyself and man peace Thou swore;
    If mercy for man now should cease,
    Then peace were exiled evermore.

MERCY. Though man has forsaken Thee by sin,
    By faith turned they to Thee once more.
    Abraham his own son would have slain,
    Whom he loved, yet he loved Thee more.

DEATH. But man is frail and constant never,
    For one good deed there are ten thousand ill.

JUSTICE. From Thy law and love turn they ever.
    Should mercy be given to them still?

GOD. Methought I showed man love,
    When first I gave them life,
    To dwell in a garden, heaven above;
    But all their work is woe and strife,
    And sin forever reigning rife.
    But, sons and daughters, hearken here;
    How might man, that has little main,
    In death's shadow, ever in fear,
    Live this life of teen and pain,
    And to Our truth true remain?

Might such a one e'er be born?
One as just as Our own law,
Who might learn all these that now be forlorn;
But in whom peace and mercy were ever sure:
Then loveday be made between ye four.
An end to bring to endless strife,
Justice, truth, mercy, peace,
Must all embrace to make this life:
So God in man shall man release.

Joachim and Anne

Province of Judea under Roman occupation. JOACHIM *and* ANNE's *house.*

JOACHIM. Blessed wife Anne, sore I dread;
Our tribe to the Temple must make offering,
Of wood to be burnt in that holy stead.
Yet for no child of us doth spring,
The priest my offering may despise,
Then great slander in the tribe of us should arise.

ANNE. Your words my heart will break in two.
We know what mercy God may us show.

JOACHIM. So let it be as He will, there is no other wise.
But this I avow to God with all the meekness I can:
If of His mercy He will a child us devise,
We shall offer it up to the Temple to be God's man.

ANNE. Thrice I kiss you with sighs full sad.
Those that part in sorrow, God make their meeting glad.

TRIBE MEMBER We be to blame if we speed not our pace.

JOACHIM. This offering for His altar with me I take,
And shall beseech, wife, before His face,
That His great mercy us merrier might make.

JOACHIM departs for the Temple.

ANNE. Now am I left alone sore may I weep.
Ah, Lord, might Ye my husband well again bring,
And from shame and sorrow might Ye him keep.
Till I see him again I cannot cease of weeping.

JOACHIM departs for the Temple.

ANNE. Now am I left alone sore may I weep.
Ah, Lord, might Ye my husband well again bring,
And from shame and sorrow might Ye him keep.
Till I see him again I cannot cease of weeping.

*At the Temple, the High Priest, REUBEN presiding. The members
of Joachim's tribe come to make offerings.*

REUBEN. Come up, sirs, and offer all now,
Ye that to make offering worthy are.

JOACHIM approaches.

Abide awhile, sir; whither wilt thou?
Thou and thy wife are barren and bare;
Neither of you fruitful never yet were.
Why dost thou among the fruitful presume and abuse?
It is a token thou art cursed there.
With great indignation thine offering I refuse.
Joachim, I charge fast from this Temple thou fare.

JOACHIM leaves the Temple.

JOACHIM. Ah, merciful Lord, what is this life?
  What have I done, Lord, to have this blame?
  For heavens I dare not go home to my wife,
  And among my neighbours I dare not abide for shame.
  I will go to my shepherds and with them abide,
  There evermore to live in sorrow and dread;
  Shame maketh many man his head for to hide.

He goes.

The hills outside the walls of Jerusalem.

SHEPHERD 1. See, Sym, see, where our brother doth stand.
  I am right glad we have him found.
  Brother, where hast thou been so long?

SHEPHERD 3. In wild woods have I been gone.
  Such healthful herbs there have I sought
  To keep our sheep from scab and rot,
  Them to save and heal.
  Lo, here be the herbs safe and sound,
  Wisely wrought for every wound –
  They would a whole man bring to the ground
  Within a little while.

  JOACHIM *comes to them.*

JOACHIM. Ha, how do ye, felas? In you is little pride.
  How fare ye and my beasts, this would I wit verily.

SHEPHERD 1. Ah, welcome hither, blessed master; we
    pasture them full wide.

SHEPHERD 3. They be lusty and fair, and greatly multiply.

SHEPHERD 2. How do ye, master? Ye look all heavily.
  How doth our dame at home? Well, I troweth?

JOACHIM. To hear ye speak of her, it slays my heart, verily.
How she doth, God himself knoweth.
The meek God lifteth up, the proud overthroweth.
Go do what ye list, see your beasts not stray.

SHEPHERD 2. After great sorrow, master, great grace ever
groweth.
Simple as we can, we shall for you pray.

JOACHIM *is left alone.*

JOACHIM. I am not worthy, Lord, upon Thee to call.
My sinful steps envenom the ground.
I, loathfullest that liveth; Thou, Lord over all.
What art Thou? Lord. What am I? Worse than a hound.
Thou hast sent me shame which my heart doth wound.
My sorrow is fearing we have done some offence:
If so, in torment let me be bound,
But spare my dear wife. I will not from hence,
But with prayers prostrate before Thee weep,
That Thou might show me here Thy presence.
My wife that will sit and sigh for my absence,
My lovingest wife, Anne, I pray Thee, Lord, keep.

ANGEL MERCY/GABRIEL *comes to* JOACHIM.

GABRIEL. Joachim, the Lord has heard your prayer,
And sends His grace to you this day:
Thy wife by thee a child shall bear.
To the Golden Gate swift make thy way.

JOACHIM. This incomparable comfort shall I never forget.
My sorrow was great, but my joy is more.
I shall home in haste, nought shall me let.
Ah, Anne, blessed be that babe of thee shall be bore.

Now farewell, my shepherds, govern you wisely.

SHEPHERD 1. Have ye good tidings, master? Then be we
glad.

JOACHIM. Praise God for me, for I am not worthy.

SHEPHERD 2. In faith, sir, we shall, since thus you have
bad.

SHEPHERD 3. I hold it helpful one of us with you gad.

JOACHIM. Nay, abide with your beasts, son, in God's
blessing.

SHEPHERD 1. We shall make us so merry, now ye be not sad
That a mile on your way shall ye hear us sing.

JOACHIM *goes.*

JOACHIM *and* ANNE'*s house.* ANNE *is in mourning.*

ANNE. Alas, for mine husband am I full woe.
I wot not on earth which way he did go.
Ah, mercy, Lord! Mercy, mercy, mercy!
Are we so sinfullest that Ye send us such sorrow?
Why do Ye thus with my husband, Lord? Why?
For my barrenness? Ye may amend this Thyself, and
Thou list, tomorrow.

She sits down beneath a tree where there is a sparrow's nest.

O Lord, what is like unto me?
Not these birds above on height,
Not the fish that swim in sea;
All these be fruitful in Thy sight:
All beasts have bounty before Thee
And only I this plight.

O Lord, what is like unto me?
Even the waters have riches rare,
And earth brings forth both herb and tree,
With fruit to taste and flowers fair;
Each thing in season praises Thee
And only I am bare.

GABRIEL *appears to her.*

GABRIEL. Anne, the Lord has heard your prayer,
And sends His blessing on your house.
A child shalt thou conceive and bear,
Whose name shall be amongst all famous.
She shall be offered into the Temple solemnly,
That of her no ill fame should spring.
And as she shall be born of a barren body,
So from her body a babe shall she bring,
That shall be the joy of all mankind.
In wedding weeds now wend thee fast,
To the Golden Gate where thou shalt find,
Thy husband hies him home at last.

ANNE. Now blessed be our Lord and all His works ay.
All heaven and earth must bless You for this.
I am so joyful I not what I may say;
There can no tongue tell what joy in me is.
To have child and husband. Who might have joys more?
I shall hie me to the gate to be there before.

She hurries away.

The Golden Gate in the walls of Jerusalem.

ANNE. Ah, blessed be our Lord, mine husband I see.
I shall on mine knees and himward creep.

JOACHIM. Ah, gracious wife Anne, now fruitful shall ye be.
  For joy of this meeting in my soul I weep.
  Have this kiss of cleanness and with you it keep.
  In God's name, now go we, wife, home to our house.

ANNE. There was never joy sank in me so deep.
  Now may we say, husband, God is to us gracious.

  They embrace.

Presentation

In the Temple.

JOACHIM. Sir prince of priests, and it please you,
  We that were barren God hath sent a child.
  To offer her to God's service we made our vow;
  Here is the same maid, Mary most mild.

REUBEN. Joachim, I have good mind how I you reviled.
  I am right joyful that God hath given you this grace.
  To be among the fruitful now be ye reconciled.

ANNE. Mary, in this holy place leave you we shall.

REUBEN. Come, sweet Mary, come; ye have a gracious face.

ANNE. In God's name, go; lo, the priest doth call.

REUBEN. Come, good Mary.

  GOD *sets his grace upon her: she dances with her feet and the
  whole house of Israel loves her.*

REUBEN. Ah, gracious Lord, this is a marvellous thing,
  That we see in this holy place:

A babe to dance of years so young;
On her the Lord has set His grace.

REUBEN *takes her and kisses her.*

To the prophetess Anna I thee commend,
So all thy cares shall she attend.

ANNE. Sweet daughter, think on your mother, Anne;
    Your parting smiteth to mine heart deep.

JOACHIM. Daughter, ye never offended God nor man.
    Loved be that Lord who doth you keep.

The Marriage of Mary and Joseph

In Nazareth.

HERALD. Oy! Unwedded men take to me tent,
    That be aught of kindred to David the king.
    The High Priest hath for you sent;
    To the Temple must ye make offering,
    Of bough or branch of some bare tree
    Each one of you. Now hasten ye.

JOSEPH. In great labour my life I lead,
    Mine occupation lieth in so many a place.
    For feebleness of age my journey I may not speed.

COUSIN 1. What cheer, Joseph? What is the case
    That ye lie here on the ground?

JOSEPH. Age and feebleness doth me unbrace,
    That I may neither well go nor stand.

COUSIN 2. The priest himself doth here command,
    That every man of David's seed
    Go to the Temple with bough in hand;
    Therefore in this journey let us proceed.

JOSEPH. Me to travel it is no need.
    I pray you, friends, go forth your way.

COUSIN 3. Yes, come forth, Joseph, I you rede,
    And knoweth what the priest will say.

COUSIN 4. I hear of a maid whose name is Mary
    Vowed to the Temple as it is told.
    Her to marry they will assay
    To some man doughty and bold.

JOSEPH. Able to be married, that is not me.
    Widow I am and evermore shall be.
    In rest and repose would I live out my life.
    And again to be married? To take a young wife?
    But to the High Priest's bidding be we all bown,
    So, neighbours and kinsmen, let us forth go.
    I take a stick in my hand and cast off my gown.
    If I fall then I shall groan with woe.
    Ye be men that may run, so go ye before.
    I am old and also cold, and would this journey were o'er.

At the Temple.

REUBEN. Sirs, from God we have this word:
    Each your boughs shall bring to me,
    He whose offering may please the Lord,
    The husband of this maid shall be.

They bring up their branches.

JOSEPH. It shall not be I, by no jot,

I shall abide behind privily.
Now would God I were home in my cot
I am ashamed to be seen, verily.

COUSIN 4. Joseph, why comest thou not to God's shrine?
As we have ours so bring up thine.
Come on, man, for shame.

JOSEPH. Ya, ya. God help. I am so aged and old
That both mine legs begin to fold –
I am nigh almost lame.

REUBEN. What! Joseph, why stand you there behind?
Iwis, sir, ye be to blame.

JOSEPH. Sir, I cannot my stick find.
To come there in truth me thinketh shame.

REUBEN. Come thence.

JOSEPH. Sir, he must lag that is near lame –
In sooth, I come as fast as I may.

REUBEN. Offer up your stick, sir, in God's name.
Why do ye not as men you pray?

JOSEPH. Now in the worship of God in heaven
I offer this stick as lily white,
And as He made the planets seven,
To His worship this work is dight.
I may not lift my hands high.
Lo, lo, lo. What see ye now?

JOSEPH's *stick flowers.*

REUBEN. Ah, mercy, mercy! Mercy, Lord, we cry.
The blessed of God we see art thou.

All cry 'Mercy'.

REUBEN. Ah, gracious God in heaven's height,
    Right wonderful Thy works be.
    Here may we see a marvellous sight:
    A dead stick beareth flowers free.
    Joseph, in heart without moan,
    Thou mayst be blithe with game and glee.
    A maid to wed thou must be gone
    By this miracle I do well see.
    Mary is her name.

JOSEPH. What! Should I wed? God forbid.
    I am an old man, so God me speed.
    And with a wife now to live in dread,
    It were neither sport nor game.

REUBEN. Against God, Joseph, thou mayst not strive.
    God wills that a wife thou have.

JOSEPH. An old man may never thrive
    With a young wife, so God me save.

REUBEN. This fair maid shall be thy wife,
    God himself her to you gave.
    What God will have, say thou not nay.

JOSEPH. Against my God I may not rave.
    Her husband and keeper will I be ay.

    MARY *and* JOSEPH *are married.*

MARY. Farewell, father and mother dear,
    From you I take my leave right here,
    God that sit in heaven so clear
    Have you in his keeping.

JOACHIM. Farewell, Mary, my sweet flower,
　　Farewell, Joseph, by God be led.

ANNE. Farewell, my child and my treasure,
　　God's grace be ever on you spread.
　　Farewell, my daughter young.

　　ANNA THE PROPHETESS *speaks to* MARY.

ANNA. On judgement day the earth shall drip sweat.
　　A king shall come from heavenly seat,
　　In flesh to judge the world with might.
　　Both good and ill shall of God have sight
　　On high with the holy when that end shall loom:
　　Flesh and souls shall wait his doom.
　　The earth be choked with briar and thorn,
　　All men's treasures turned to scorn.
　　Angels then shall quake with fear,
　　And all the earth be turned to fire.
　　Shall nothing here on earth be kenned
　　But it shall be strewed and brend,
　　All waters and the sea.
　　Then shall both hill and dale
　　Run together, great and small,
　　And all shall even be.
　　At his coming shall trumpets blast.
　　That no man that may hear it,
　　Be he never so steadfast
　　But shall he quake for all his wit.
　　Then shall earth gape and grin
　　With rivers of fire and burning rock,
　　That men may know their doom therein,
　　When God shall every heart unlock.

Annunciation

JOSEPH *and* MARY's *house.*

JOSEPH. Now, listen well, Mary, what I tell thee:
　　I must go out hence far thee fro.
　　I will go labour in far country,
　　In truth to maintain our household so.
　　We are not rich in worldly thing,
　　And yet of our sustenance we shall not miss.
　　Therefore abide ye at home to your pleasing;
　　To worship your God is all your bliss.

MARY. I pray to God He speed your way,
　　And in soul-health He may you keep,
　　And send you wealth both night and day;
　　He shield and save you in wake or sleep.

JOSEPH *goes.*

GABRIEL *comes to* MARY.

GABRIEL. Hail, most favored, the Lord is with thee.
　　Among all women blessed shalt thou be.

MARY *is deeply disturbed.*

GABRIEL. Ne dread ye not Mary mild,
　　In God grace have ye over all;
　　Thou shalt conceive and bear a child
　　His name Jesu shalt thou call.
　　Mickel of might then shall he be,
　　He shall be great and called man's Son.
　　As king forever reign shall he,
　　Of his kingdom and dignity
　　Shall no man earthly know nor con.

MARY. In what manner of wise shall this be?
  For knowing of man have I none now.

GABRIEL. God's Spirit shall come from above to thee,
  The virtue of Him highest shall thee overshadow.
  For see, Elizabeth, thy cousin clean,
  The which was barren and past all age,
  And now with child has she been
  Six months and more, as well is seen;
  Nothing is impossible to God's usage.

  MARY *bows her head.*

MARY. Behold, the handmaiden of the Lord:
  Be it unto me after thy word.

  GABRIEL *leaves and* MARY *conceives.*

Salutation

ELIZABETH*'s house.*

MARY *arrives.*

ELIZABETH. Mary, my child, come near, come near.

MARY. God bless thee, Elizabeth, my cousin dear.

  They embrace and kiss. ELIZABETH *cries out.*

ELIZABETH. Ah, what wonder thing is this!
  When, sweet Mary, thou didst me kiss,
  The child stirred in my body
  For great joy of thy company
  And the babe beneath thy heart.

Mary, blessed thou art:
Through thee God fulfills His word.

MARY. Who am I, I ask Thee, Lord,
That all the earth should bless me so?

MARY *weeps*.

ELIZABETH. Comfort, good Mary, thou shouldst have mirth.

MARY. What this may mean, I do not know;
I am the simplest creature on this earth.

ELIZABETH. Sweet Mary, rise up. I beseech thee, come.
I say thou should not hasten home,
But in this house shalt take thy rest,
Until Joseph, the far fields from,
Doth he return. This think I best.

Joseph's Doubt

MARY *and* JOSEPH's *house.* MARY *is visibly pregnant.*

JOSEPH. How, dame, how! Undo your door, undo.
Are ye at home? Why speak ye nought?

MARY. Joseph, my husband, why cry ye so?

JOSEPH. For to come in is all my thought.

MARY *lets* JOSEPH *in.*

JOSEPH. Ow, dame, how is this meant?
Thy womb is great, it ginneth to rise.
Then hast thou begun a sinful guise.
Tell now me now in what wise

Thyself thou hast shent?
Say, Mary, this child's father, who is?
I pray thee tell me, and that anon.

MARY. The Father of heaven and ye it is —
I did never forfeit with any man.
This child is God's and your.

JOSEPH. God's child! Thou liest, in fay.
God did never jape so with maids.
And I came never there, I dare well say,
Yet so nigh thy bower.
But yet I say, Mary, whose child is this?

MARY. God's and your, I say, iwis.

JOSEPH. Alas, alas, my name is shent.
All men may me now despise.
Thou foolish wench, while I was went,
Hath list to some lewd lurdeyn's lies.
Dame, why didst thou so?
For this sin that thou hast do
I thee forsake and from thee go

MARY. Alas, dear husband, amend your mood.
The Son of man in flesh and blood
Shall of your wife be born.
Forsooth, the angel, thus said she,
That God would send this child to me,
To save all that is forlorn.

JOSEPH. An angel? Fie, fie for shame.
Ye sin now in that ye say,
To put an angel in so great blame.
No, no. Let be. Do way!
It was some boy began this game

That clothed was clean and gay.
And ye give him now an angel's name.
To hide the truth from me is vain,
The child-bearing may thou not hide.
Sit thou still here till I come again,
I have an errand here beside.

He goes from her.

MARY. Ah, gracious God in heaven's throne,
    Comfort me in this hard case.
    Merciful God, amend his moan,
    As I did never so great trespass.

    JOSEPH *alone.*

JOSEPH. Alas, why is it so?
    To the priests I should this tell,
    That they the law may her do,
    With stones then her to quell.
    Nay, nay, yet God forbid,
    That I should do so vengeful deed.
    Until I wist well why.
    I never knew of her, so God me speed,
    Token of thing in word or deed
    That touched villainy.

    GABRIEL *comes to* JOSEPH.

GABRIEL. Joseph, Joseph, thou weepest shrill.
    From thy wife why comest thou out?

JOSEPH. I pray thee, let me weep my fill;
    Go forth thy way and let me not.

GABRIEL. In thy weeping thou dost right ill –
    Against God thou hast miswrought.

Go cheer thy wife with hearty will,
And change thy cheer, amend thy thought.
She is a maiden ay.
The Son of man will of her be born,
And she clean maid as she was before,
To save mankind, that is forlorn.
Go cheer her, therefore, I say.

JOSEPH. Say, what art thou? Tell me this thing.

GABRIEL. I Gabriel am; God's mercy I,
That have taken Mary to my keeping.
Thou must of her no sin imply.

JOSEPH. For thy great comfort I thank thee
That thou hast sent me this space.
I might well have wist that she
Would never have done trespass.

He returns to MARY.

JOSEPH. Ah mercy, mercy, my gentle make,
Mercy, I have said amiss.
All that I have said, here I forsake.
Your sweet feet now let me kiss.

MARY. Nay, let be my feet, not those ye take;
My mouth ye may kiss, iwis,
And welcome unto me.

They kiss.

JOSEPH. Gramercy, Mary, my own sweet wife.
Thy child and thee shall I ward from strife.
I make this vow to thee.

Simeon

Evening in the Court of Women at the Temple. The gates have not yet been closed.

SIMEON. I have been priest in Jerusalem here
    And taught Thine law many a year,
    Desiring in all my mind
    That the time were drawing near
    In which Thy Saviour should appear
    On earth to save mankind.
    Ah, good God in majesty,
    How long shall I abide Thee
    Till that Thou the Saviour doth send,
    That I on earth might him see?
    Good Lord, consider to me –
    I draw fast to an end –
    That, ere my strengths from me wend,
    Good Lord, send the Son of man,
    That I with my full mind
    Might worship him if I can.

ANGEL PEACE. Simeon, leave thy careful steven,
    For thy prayer is heard in heaven.
    The Oil of Mercy cometh nigh,
    And thou shalt see it ere thou die,
    Here in the Temple thou dwellest in.
    The darkness of original sin
    He shall make light and clarify.
    And now the deeds shall begin,
    Which promised were by prophecy.

SIMEON. Ah, I thank Thee, Lord of grace,
    That hath granted me time and space

To live and see this.
And I will bide now in this place
Where I may see the Son's face,
Which is my joy and bliss.

The Prophetess ANNA *comes to* SIMEON.

ANNA. All hail, Simeon, what tidings with you?
   Why make ye all this mirth now?

SIMEON. Anna, and ye wist how,
   So should ye, I make avow,
   And all manner of men that are.
   The Son of man, mankind to mend,
   Cometh now to cease our care.
   I shall him see ere my life's end.

The bells start to ring.

ANNA. Ah, dear God, what noise is there?
   The bells ring in a solemn tone.

SIMEON. Such a noise heard I never ere;
   The bells ring by their own.

ANNA. Listen, ye deaf. See, ye blind.
   For thus the day of the Lord is signed.

SIMEON. Mercy is come and vengeance is past,
   And God shall bring us bliss at last.

On the Road to Bethlehem

JOSEPH. Lief spouse, when I did look a little while
   Your face me seemed full sad;

Yet now I see that ye do smile.
Why be thou here both sore and glad?

MARY. Two peoples with mine eyes I see.
Some there are both blithe and merry,
Yet other some are sighing and sorry;
I wit not wherefore this should be.

JOSEPH. Poor men's wealth is ever in doubt.
Alas, that thus we must wend out
This tribute now to pay.
I won no good this seven year,
And now here comes this emperor
To get all that he may.

MARY *gasps and the vault of heaven stands still, the air is in amazement and the birds are motionless in the sky. On the earth, men eat but do not eat, sheep are driven but remain still, the shepherd raises his hand but does not strike, the mouths of kid goats bend to the flow of the river but do not drink. Only* JOSEPH *sees all this. Then everything goes on its course.*

MARY. Husband, I know right well
The babe will be born, this truth I feel.
In this place shall be the birth;
Between my sides I feel he stirreth.

JOSEPH. God be thine help, spouse, it pains me sore.
How should he be born in place so poor?
There is no house, nor yet a wall;
Fire nor wood none here is.

MARY. Joseph, mine husband, abide here I shall,
For here will be born the Son of bliss.
Avoid you hence our of this place,
Here shall I abide God's high grace.

JOSEPH. Already, wife, you for to please
  I will go hence out of your way,
  And seek some midwives you for to ease
  When that ye travail of child this day.
  Farewell, true wife, I love thee ay;
  To God's comfort now I leave thee.

MARY. To God in heaven for you I pray,
  He you preserve whereso ye be.

  JOSEPH *goes*.

MARY. My God, my God, that all has wrought,
  I would now die and pass to nought.

  The baby is born.

Midwives

The place where MARY *has given birth.*

JOSEPH *approaches*.

JOSEPH. Mary, how dost thou fare? Tell me thy cheer.

  MARY *laughs*.

JOSEPH. Why do ye laugh, wife, tell me this?
  Two good midwives have I brought here.

MARY. Husband, take it not amiss,
  Though I laugh and great joy have.
  Here is the child by God begot,
  Born now of me, that all thing shall save.

JOSEPH. I ask your grace, I saw him not.

O gracious child, I welcome thee.
(*To the Midwives.*) My wife and child come see, come see.

SALOME. Sweet sister, how fare ye in this place?

MARY. I thank the Father of His high grace,
   I am well and my child is born.

ZELOMY. Who was the midwife of this fair child?

MARY. He that nothing will have forlorn
   Sent me this babe, and I maid mild.

ZELOMY. With hand let me now touch and feel
   If ye have need of medicine.
   I shall you comfort and help right well
   As other women if ye have pain.

MARY. Pain nor grieving felt I none.

   ZELOMY *examines* MARY.

ZELOMY. Come near, good sister Salome.
   Behold the breasts of this clean maid,
   Full of fair milk how that they be,
   And her child clean, as ye may see;
   Not as others are, foul arrayed,
   But clean and pure both mother and child.
   Of this matter I am dismayed,
   To see them both thus undefiled.

SALOME. It is not true. I will not believe
   Till with my hand I have assayed,
   In my conscience it may never cleave
   That she hath a child and is a maid.

   She examines MARY.

Mine hand is dead and dry as clay –
Alas the time that I was born,
My hand's power is now all lorn,
Stiff as a stick, and may not plight.

GABRIEL. Woman, thy sorrow for to spite
Touch the clothes where he lies, tite.
For all that sicken may he restore.

SALOME *touches the baby's cloth. Her hand is restored.*

SALOME. Ah, blessed be He for evermore.
My hand is healed by this child.
Of this blessed babe my leave I take,
And also of you, his mother mild,
Of this great miracle more knowledge to make.

The Midwives depart.

Visit of the Shepherds and the Wise Men

The Shepherds come to MARY *and the baby.*

AARON. Here he is.

DAW. Who shall go before?

GIB. I ne reck, by my hair.

AARON. Ye are of the old store,
It seems you iwis.

GIB. An angel brought us tidings new
A babe in Bethlem should be born –

AARON. Of whom has spoke our prophecy true –

GIB. And bad us seek him here this morn.

AARON. The angel said that he should save
This world and all that dwell therein.

GIB. Therefore if we should ought after crave,
To worship him I will begin.
Hail, young child! Here I offer,
If thou would receive,
Little is that I have;
This will I vouchsave –
A small spruce coffer.

AARON. Hail, sovereign saviour, for thou hast us sought!
Hail, freely food and flower, a cup have I brought
To my bairn.
Hail, little tiny mop!
Of our creed thou art crop;
I would drink from thy cup,
Little day-star.

DAW. Hail, darling dear, Son of man indeed
I pray thee be near when that I have need.
Hail, sweet is thy cheer! My heart would bleed
To see thee sit here in so poor weed.
Take my pipe small.
Were I on rock or valley below,
This pipe, my bairn, I could blow,
That all the world about should know
And shake as it should fall.

MARY *treasures all these things and ponders them in her heart.*

GIB. Farewell, fair child, with thy mother also.

AARON. We shall this record where e'er we go.

DAW. That all be restored – God grant it so.

GIB. Amen to that word. Sing we thereto
　　On height.
　　To joy all sam,
　　With mirth and game,
　　To the laud of this lamb.
　　Sing we this night.

The SHEPHERDS *depart, singing.*

JOSEPH. Mary, I marvel for my part,
　　How of our child these folk do preach.

MARY. Yea, Joseph, in my heart
　　I bear full still their speech.

The WISE MEN *arrive. They all speak in their own tongues.*

WISE MAN 2. We seek a bairn that all shall bield,
　　His certain sign hath said us so,
　　And his mother, a maiden mild,
　　Here hope we to find them two.

JOSEPH. Come near, good sirs, and see,
　　Your way to end is brought;
　　Behold here sirs, hear and see
　　The same that ye have sought.

WISE MAN 3. Lofed be that Lord that lasts ay,
　　That has guided us thus courteously.

WISE MAN 2. Let us make now no more delay,
　　But tite take forth our treasury.

WISE MAN 1. He shall be king, clean and wise,
　　So here I praise him as best I may
　　With gold that is greatest of price;
　　Be pleased with this present I pray.

WISE MAN 2. Since thou o'er us all shall sit,
    As priest most high in heavenly throne
    Incense to thy service is fit;
    Take it and make us thine own.

WISE MAN 3. And since thy body buried shall be,
    This myrrh I give to thy graving.
    The gift is not great of degree,
    Receive it, and see to our saving.

WISE MAN 1. For solace sere now may we sing,
    All is performed that we for prayed;
    But, good bairn, give us thy blessing,
    For fair hap is before thee laid.

WISE MAN 2. Wend we now to Herod the king
    For of this point he will be paid,
    And come himself and make offering
    Unto this same, for so he said.

    GABRIEL *appears and directs them another way.*

Herod

The Palace of KING HEROD THE GREAT, *recently appointed 'King of the Jews' by the Romans.* HEROD *and* ANTIPAS, *his son, are consulting Torah scrolls. His soldiers are on hand.*

HEROD. Great God, methink I brast for anger and for
    teen;
    I trow those wise men be past, that here with us has been.
    They promised me full fast ere now here to be seen,
    I tell you.
    That boy they said they sought,

With offering that they brought;
It moves my heart right nought
To break his neck in two.

ANTIPAS. Certes, father, here find I
Well written in a prophecy,
How that the prophet Isay
(That never beguiled)
Tells that a maiden of her body
Shall bear a child;
The child shall hight Emmanuel.
All as the wise men did us tell.
This other says thus, list if ye may,
In Bethlem a gracious lord shall spray,
That of Jewry mighteous king shall be ay,
And him shall honour
Both king and emperor.

HEROD. Should I cower him before?
Shall he have more power than I?
Ah, wellaway!
Out, alas! For dole I die
Long ere my day.
Whereto wear I a crown?
Or am called of great renown?
I am the foulest borne down
That ever was man;
And namely by a foul swalchon
That no good can.
My name springs far and near, the doughtiest, men
    me call;
What joy is me to hear a lad to seize my stall?
If I this crown may bear, that boy shall buy for all.

As I am king in land
I shall with this steel brand
Break all his bones.

To his SOLDIERS.

To Bethlem look ye go, and all the land about;
All boy bairns to slay; of all that rout
Alive leave none that lies in swaddle-clout,
I rede you.
Spare no kins blood,
Let all run on flood
And women wax wood;
I warn you, sirs, to speed you.

The SOLDIERS *go.*

Flight

GABRIEL *comes to* JOSEPH.

GABRIEL. Awake, Joseph, and take intent.
Thou rise and sleep no more.
If thou will save thy son unshent,
Full fast must ye now fare.
Herod the king will do to dead
All boy-bairns in every stead
That by Bethlehem be
Upon this tide.

JOSEPH. Alas, full woe is me.
Where shall we hide?

GABRIEL. Thereof have thou no dread;

Wend forth, and leave thy din,
The way He shall you lead,
The Lord of all mankin.

GABRIEL *goes*.

JOSEPH. Mary, my darling dear,
  I am full woe for thee.

MARY. Ah, lief Joseph, what cheer?

JOSEPH. The cheer of me is done for ay.

MARY. Alas, what tidings heard have ye?

JOSEPH. Now certes, full ill to thee to say,
  There is nought else but we must flee

MARY. Lief Joseph, why?

JOSEPH. That young lad's life thou must forego
  Lest we fast flee his foe.

MARY. His foe? I dark, I dare,
  Who may my care
  Of bales end?
  To flee I would full fain,
  For all this world to gain,
  I would not see him slain.
  Who would my small son shend?

JOSEPH. I warn thee, he is sorely threat
  By Herod king, hard harms to have.
  With that youngling if we be met
  There is no salve that him may save.
  I warn thee well, Herod slays all
  Boy-bairns, both great and small.

MARY. Lief Joseph, who told you this?

JOSEPH. The angel Mercy that came from bliss
    Wakened me out of my sleep
    That comely child from cares to keep.

MARY. To slay this bairn I bare,
    What wight in world had will?

JOSEPH. Now, lief Mary, be still.
    This helps us ne'er.
    It is no boot to greet,
    Truly without train;
    Our trail it may not beat
    But well more make our pain.

MARY. Alas, how should I let?
    My son that is so sweet
    Is sought for to be slain.

JOSEPH. The best wise that we may
    Haste us out of here.
    There is nought else to say
    But tite pack up our gear.

MARY. Alas, Joseph, for woe,
    Was never wight in world so ill.

JOSEPH. Do way, Mary, and say not so,
    For thou shall have no cause theretill.
    For wit thou well, God is our friend,
    He will be with us whereso we wend.

    They go.

Slaughter of the Innocents

'A voice is heard in Ramah,
Lamenting and weeping bitterly:
It is Rachel weeping for her children,
Refusing to be comforted for her children
Because they are no more.'

Jeremiah

HEROD's *Palace.*

HEROD. Ah, God abown,
    So light is my soul,
    That all sugar is my gall.
    I may do what I shall
    And bear up my crown.
    I was cast in care, so frightly afraid –
    But I need not despair, for low is he laid
    That I most dread ere, so have I him flayed.

    Now, kind knights, be merry and glad,
    With much diligence show ye some mirth.
    For, by great God, more mirth never I had,
    Nor was in more joy since the time of my birth.
    For my foe is dead, dashed as a toad.
    There is no king above me here on earth.
    Mirth, therefore, make ye, and be nothing sad.
    Spare neither meat nor drink, and spare for no dearth
    Of wine or bread.
    For I am king alone
    So worthy be there none,
    Therefore be merry everyone,
    For now my foe is dead.

The feast is prepared.

SOLDIER 1. When the boys sprawled at my spear's end,
By God I thee swear, it was a goodly sight.
A good game it was that boy for to shend
That would have been our king and put you from your
right.

SOLDIER 2. Now truly, my lord the king, we had been
unkind,
And never none of us able to be a knight,
If that any of us to them had been a friend
And saved any life against thy mickle might,
From death them to flit.

HEROD. Amongst all that great rout,
He is dead, I have no doubt.
Therefore, son, round about,
Blow up a merry fit.

DEATH *appears to* HEROD.

Purification

At the Temple.

MARY. Good Simeon, receive of me
This offering of turtles two,
As falls, sir, to your degree
And is to this office due.

SIMEON *takes the child in his arms and kisses it.*

He hands the baby back to MARY.

SIMEON. Mary, I shall say the truth ere ye go.
   This was put here to win us from woe.
   But the sword of sorrow thy heart shall drill,
   When thou shalt see soothly thy son suffer ill,
   For the weal of all wretches that shall be his will.
   Now let me die, Lord, and hence pass,
   For I, Thy servant in this place
   Have seen my Saviour dear,
   Which Thou hast ordained before the face
   Of all mankind this time of grace
   Openly to appear.
   To be a light shining clear
   To those that dwell in death's darkness;
   To be the glory of Thy people here,
   And lead us in the way of peace.

DEATH *appears.*

End of Part One.